How To Fart – Louder, Longer, and Stronger...without soiling your undies!

Also learn how to fart on command, fart more often, and increase the smell.

by Dr R. Sole Ph.D.

Table of Contents

About the Author

Introduction

ABOUT THE AUTHOR

The author graduated with honors from the Flatulence Academy of Research and Training (F.A.R.T.) in 1999 and gained his honorary doctorate in 2006 at the Southern Holistic Institute of Technology (S.H.I.T.).

Dr R. Sole Ph.D. (Pooh Hole Diploma) is internationally regarded as the world's foremost expert on farts and farting. From his humble Tasmanian Underground Research Dept. (T.U.R.D.), he conducts groundbreaking research and development on the science of Farts. His works have been regularly published in such distinguished scientific publications as Scientific

Farter, and What Fart is That? He is currently hopeful of obtaining an Australian Government grant from the dept. of clean air so he can delve even deeper into a topic he has devoted his whole life to. Dr R. Sole is a passionate farter and is world renowned for his abilities to coach and train others. He is excited to be presenting this roll up your sleeves, hands on shitty gritty guide to all those who wish to follow in his footsteps...although he warns not to stand too close.

INTRODUCTION:

There are many books on the market giving solutions on how to stop farting. But what is there for people who want to fart more? To fart louder? To fart longer? To fart stronger...both pressure wise, and smell wise? Those that want to become champions at passing wind? Those that want to exercise their right to free speech, and exercise their sphincters at the same time? Those who say to hell with the clean air bill? And to those who want to fart responsibly, and not leave skid marks. And to those that just want to have fun!

Well, to all those people, this book is written for you!

In this concise, no fluff (well, actually full of fluff and hot air) report you'll learn to do exactly what the book title says...

Fart louder, longer and stronger. In this short read you'll learn to build up the fart pressure with scientific food combining, and how to release it at will with advanced bowel control. Impress your friends, relatives, and partners. You'll be the talk of the town. Learn to create copious amounts of wind, and how to utilize it for best effect. You'll learn how to generate the gas, how to control and propel it, and how to make it smell beastly! From meek and mild through too big, bold and offensive…in fact deadly!

Use these skills to clear a long bank queue, get a seat on a crowded train or bus, get extra leg room on a long flight, in fact the possibilities are endless. Go into stealth mode and watch people give each other the hairy eye ball as they try to figure out who dropped the clanger. Movie theatres, restaurants, amusement rides…nothing is safe…nothing is out of bounds. Get creative!

Use your new found super powers to go above and beyond what others thought possible. Use shock and awe tactics. Singe peoples nose hairs. Create havoc. Have them gagging, and gasping for air.

But with these new found powers comes great responsibility. Use them for good. Clear a bus to make a seat for a little old lady…and let someone else take the blame! (Insert evil chuckle here). Everything and anything is possible in this new paradigm of achievement that you will find your life propelled into. Blast yourself into success. Rise to heights and levels previously unimaginable. The world truly is your oyster, or perhaps I should say pickled egg. Forget about dropping your lunch, that will all be behind you…think about dropping a whole shopping trolley of cheese, tasty!

You will now be a famed *Fartiste*, and the envy of your colleagues, friends, and work mates. Walk tall, with your nose held high. You will exude a presence that commands attention. At last, gain the respect you deserve.

Part I

FART FUEL

Fueling the beast. It's all about chemistry. What we want to do is combine foods that will create a chemical reaction to produce wind. This is the easiest way by far of improving your farting ability.

And this is the part where you make them strong, in regards to smell.

I've put together an Olfactory (stinkiness) SCALE, and depending on what strength you want to go to, you can select the appropriate foods or formula from the menu.

Olfactory (stinkiness) SCALE

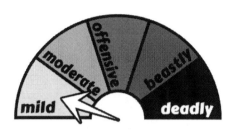

Well, you might be saying by now fancy fart-meter scales are all well and good, but how does that relate to practical everyday situations? I'm so glad you asked! The following pictures demonstrate the scale of stinkiness on a very practical level. Take for instance an everyday event of waiting for a bus.

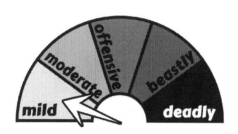

Standing on the right at the bus stop you see an innocent looking young lad, by the name of Fartus Maximus, but known to his friends as Max. But don't let that innocent look fool you. Inside something much more sinister is brewing. Max is a Master Farter. And he has just gently eased out a mild level one, Bubbler. The boy next to him suspects something rotten is going down, but the others are so far oblivious to the lurking danger that awaits them.

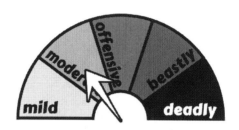

In this next scene, Max has upped the ante slightly, and popped out a moderate level 2, One Cheek Sneak. Notice how he is leaning ever so slightly to the side, to facilitate this well executed but subtle operation. Everyone at the bus stop is conscious that something is going down, but is still not aware of the threat that lies ahead.

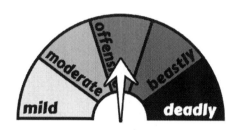

As you can see now, things are heating up! Max has gone on the offensive, and it's starting to really hit the spot. He has released a level 3 Scud. The people in the bus shelter are wishing they were on a plane instead, where oxygen masks would now be dropping down. Note Max's expression, he's starting to enjoy himself now, he knows a fart is better out than in…and he has plenty, and loves to share them!

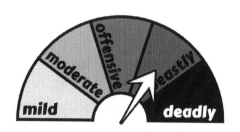

10

Alarm bells are really starting to ring for everyone now, but they have left it too late to get away. Their limbs are starting to stiffen, their nostril hairs, to singe, and their stomachs are on the verge of going into uncontrollable convulsions. He has just released a level 4, Chemical Choker. Max is reveling in his accomplishment, and basking in the ambience...he's got them just where he wants, and yet the best (worst) is still to come...

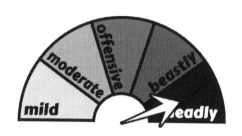

...the deadly Atomic fart. Max has dropped the dreaded Dirty Bomb, one of the most lethal farts ever developed. The fallout is catastrophic. Everyone is knocked out cold. And when the bus comes, guess who's guaranteed a seat!

PRIMING THE PUMP:

Generally, beans, high fiber grains, fruits, and most vegetables (especially cauliflower and broccoli) work the best for most people. The most spectacular results are often obtained in the first week of switching to a vegetarian diet from a meat eating one.

After that the results diminish as your body gets used to the new diet. At this point it's good to switch back again. But during that first week, you can expect to produce copious amounts of gas, resulting in an impressive 100 plus farts per day.

There are two basic food types when it comes to fart power nutrition.

Volumizers, and Vomitizers.

Volumizers are what control the amount of gas you produce. Too much and you'll get a belly ache. Not enough and you won't be able to sustain the pressure needed for a good long fart. This is necessary for auditory fulfillment and satisfaction.

Vomitizers control the amount of smell. The higher the vomitizer score, indicated on the fart-meter, the more pungent the odor, and the more likely those around you will gag because of the vial stench. This is what gives you olfactory fulfillment and nasal satisfaction. (see earlier pic of level 4 fart on page 10)

Here is a list of the best foods for powering your farts.

NOTE: Because of individual differences in body chemistry (digestive enzymes, bacteria etc.) these foods might not apply to everybody. Experiment to fine tune what works best for your physiology.

A-Z FART FUEL SUPER FOODS			
Apples	Apricots	Beans	Bran
Broccoli	Brussels sprouts	Cabbage	Carrots
Cauliflower	Dairy products	Eggplant	Nuts
Onions	Peaches	Pears	Popcorn
Prunes	Raisins	Soybean	Tuna

Sulfur is the secret sauce!

A little lesson in chemistry. The gas that really makes farts smell obnoxious is hydrogen sulfide (H_2S). Hydrogen sulfide is known as the rotten egg gas. Our bodies will create more of this gas when we mix high sulfur content foods, with foods high in hydrogen, since these foods supply the raw ingredient to form H_2S.

Olfactory shock modulation (regulating the pong)

Getting creative… This knowledge will enable you to tweak the consistency of the gas so that either more or less hydrogen sulfide (H_2S) is produced. Through this, you will be able to control your level of stinkiness from mild, right through to deadly on the Fart-Meter scale (see page 3).

Beefing up the pong (let the magic begin)...

Since foods high in sulfur are what provide the key ingredient for pong, it pays to know what they are.

TABLE OF THE TOP
SULFUR CONTAINING FOODS

Meat is one of the best sources of sulfur. One of the key ingredients found in amino acids in meats is sulfur. Chicken, turkey, beef, pork, rabbit, most fish, and goat, are all meat sources that are very high in sulfur.

Eggs are a great source of sulfur. Chicken eggs, particularly the yolks, are rich in sulfur.

The Allium genus group of foods includes seasonings such as chive, onion, garlic, leek, and shallot. These foods contain compounds such as allyl sulfides and sulfoxides and this group of foods is one of the very best sources of sulfur!

Vegetables contain glucosinolates which are sulfur rich nutrients. Edamame beans are the highest in sulfur. Other vegetables that are high in sulfur are other beans, peas, sweet corn, spinach, mustard greens, broccoli, cauliflower, cabbage, bamboo shoots, kale, asparagus, kohlrabi, okra, eggplant and lettuce.

Avocado is the fruit (yes, it is a fruit, not a vegetable!) that is highest in sulfur content, followed by kiwi fruit, banana, pineapple and strawberry.

Grapefruit, melon, grape, peach and orange are also high in sulfur.

Other foods that are high in sulfur include chocolate, milk, milk products, tea, coffee, grains, cashew nut, sesame seed, pistachio nut, peanut, and other nuts.

Now if you don't want to go to extreme changes in your eating habits, I've put together this quick fix solution of formulas. These are your shortcuts that will quickly and easily get you propelled on your exciting new journey...

FORMULA 1: Fart Fuel Wrap

INGREDIENTS:

Quart sized liquid egg whites carton
(Or whole eggs…definitely more fart power as far
as gas volume goes using just the whites, but if
you're after smell, go for whole eggs. The sulfur
contained in the yolks is what performs the magic).
Pinto beans
Rice
Whole wheat Tortilla
Soymilk

DIRECTIONS:

Fry the contents of at least half the carton of
egg whites, mix with a can of pinto beans and
some rice, and wrap in a whole wheat tortilla and
wash it all down with a large glass of soymilk.
Wait a couple of hours and let 'em rip…
CAUTION: May result in a Wet One or two.
Practice at home first before taking to the streets.

FORMULA 2: Quick Stink

Vanilla whey protein powder mixed with warm milk.
4-6 slices of whole grain bread

This is aptly named the Quick Stink because it's so quick and easy to put together. Don't be fooled by its elegant simplicity though, for some people this will have a kick like a mule.

FORMULA 3: Fast and Furious

Whey protein shake (any flavor, mixed with milk)
Baked beans, steamed cabbage, broccoli and brussels sprouts.

Although fast to prepare, don't underestimate the fury this little beauty can release in your bowels.

FORMULA 4: Super Stench

Baked beans, broccoli, garlic, and eggs. Protein bar (the sugar alcohols contained within them provide the magic) or protein shake with milk.

This is a wolf in sheep's clothing. It doesn't look much on paper, but there's a real beast lurking below the surface, just waiting for you to unleash its stench with your digestive juices.

FORMULA 5: Two Veg Surprise

Brussels sprouts, cabbage, beef with mushrooms
3 grams sulfur powder or tablets

Once again, don't let simplicity be mistaken for ineffectiveness. Like the name suggests, this little baby holds a delightful surprise. Perfect if you're thinking of lighting it up, be careful around naked flames.

BONUS FORMULA: Fart powder

1 ounce Glucose
2 ounces Licorice Powder
1 ounce sweet whey powder
3 grams MSM sulfur powder
…then just add to a hot drink of milk. (either cow's or soy)

Take extreme care with this one; remember we don't want you spray painting your undies. Proceed with caution. Just do a little test release first before attempting any big blasts. Don't say I didn't warn you! If all goes well the first time, for added adventure and excitement, you may want to increase the quantity to two serves (two glasses) next time.

FOUR USEFUL TIPS

TIP 1: chewing gum is a great way to improve your farting prowess because it animates the digestive system and makes you swallow more air than usual.

TIP 2: Consume lots of carbs
Of the three main nutrients (protein, carbohydrates, fats), carbohydrates produce the most gas since starch and sugar easily ferment. About 50% of the population is equipped with bacteria that particularly prefer munching on unprocessed carbohydrates. As you might already know, beans contain more indigestible carbohydrates than most foods.

TIP 3: Consume lots of indigestible food
Many daily foods are considered "indigestible" — milk is considered one of them for people who are lactose intolerant. Lactose intolerance means the body is unable to digest milk sugar, so it sets it aside as waste.
If you are lactose intolerant and happen to have a lot of "gas enzymes" in your digestive system, milk will be a fantastic fart fuel for you.

TIP 4: Know your enzymes
Because of differences in composition of each person's intestinal fauna; people do not necessarily react similarly to the same foods. For instance, 2 people can eat a meal rich in indigestible carbohydrates, and only one of them can develop gas. This is because his or her intestinal tract contains more fart creating enzymes. This explains why one person may claim that apples or onions give them wind, while others claim not to be affected. It is dependent on the type and amount of bacteria in the large intestine.

Part II
CONTROLLING YOUR MOTIONS

Now in this lesson, we're going to build upon what you learned about gassing up in part one. This is quite advanced, very few people know about this. But if you can master it, it will take your ability to fart to the next level. You will become a Master Farter! The Yoda of farts...or perhaps that should be yodeler of Farts.

No one will be able to come close to you...quite literally! And you will be able to give Max a run for his money.

OK, what this lesson involves is the physical technique of amplifying your results. It will enable you to be able to fart on command. And for best results, you combine with the lessons learned in part one of this book. Word of warning though, while you've still got your "L" plates on and are learning, practice the lessons separately at first, we don't want any accidents or unpleasant surprises (ie. A Shart…a fart with a lump in it!).

NOTE: the all–time Master of this was a Frenchman by the name of Joseph Le Petomane who over a century ago performed his unique act on stage in front of packed audiences. Le Petomane could draw in huge amounts of air or water at will through his back door and expel at will to perform a number of spectacular feats.

He could blow out candles (from a distance of a foot) or to shoot jets of water…sucked in immediately beforehand…as far as four or five yards. He could play recognizable tunes.

Le Petomane would insert a rubber hose into his backside and, with a cigarette inserted into the hose's free end, smoke it! To do his rectal smoking he used his sphincter alternately breathing in and exhaling. He could also play a flute this way too!

I kid you not, just Google his name. But you are best going to Amazon and getting the original book of this famous Fartiste, complete with genuine photograph.(http://amzn.to/17xszXy).

Part 1 of this book (which deals with food chemistry) is by far the easiest technique, but technique 2, although a little tough at first, is well worth the effort because if you learn to do it right you'll be able to let rip with the most super loud and long farts you've ever heard, whenever you want!

You'll never be bored again! Maybe embarrassed at times, but never bored! What a great way to entertain your friends!

The easiest way to learn this technique is to either

1) Kneel and lean forward with your elbows on the floor, bringing your backside above your head

or…

2) Lie on your back and bring your knees towards your chest.

In the practice of Yoga, positions or postures are known as Asanas. In the science of Flatulence, these two positions or postures are known as "Ass-anas".

While in either of these positions, try to relax the muscles around your abdomen and butt. When you do it correctly, you'll feel a small, steady flow of air entering your backside. Holding your nose and breath at the same time, will cause the air to rush in faster. Using your free hand to pull one of your cheeks apart will help too.

After a few seconds of "inhaling" like this, your body will get the urge to blow it back out...and you'll fart!

Here's a demonstration video of position one in action...http://bit.ly/19oO6DT

Now I have to warn you, this takes practice. Most people cannot do it at first. But don't give up! People who master this technique can let out the most outrageously long and loud farts you've ever heard! I'm talking about 30 to 90 seconds, and even longer.

As your skill develops, and you get the "feel" for the technique, you will no longer need to go into the conspicuous learning positions above.

You'll enter "stealth" mode, and be able to do it sitting or standing, so you'll be able to surprise people anywhere, at any time!

And at this stage you can take it to the next level by combining the foods you learned about in part one, with the physical technique you have just learned in this lesson.

Part III

CONCLUSION
GO FORTH AND FART

Putting it all together. This is about taking your skills out to the world!

You know what to eat.

You know how to supercharge it.

You may want to wear some adult diapers the first few times you practice in public.

Remember, our goal is to fart louder, longer, and stronger…without soiling your undies.

Learn which foods work best for you by experimenting. Once you know the best ones for your particular body chemistry, eat more of them.

Use this information wisely. With knowledge comes great power and responsibility. Serve the world goodly and well, serve them with the loudest, longest, strongest and smelliest farts you can. Use this knowledge for the greater good. Go forth and fart!

Special Bonus Chapter
COMPETITION FARTING

For those who want to take this to the next level, and start entering and winning fart competitions, here are a few tips.

Let it brew. Don't let it go as soon as you feel it coming on. Many women fall into this trap. They just let their farts slowly seep out, whenever they first feel them. You need to give them time to cook, to build pressure. No wonder women are generally lousy farters when compared to guys. I'm not being sexist, this is just a fact.

The brewing process will achieve 4 highly desirable outcomes…

1) The fart will be much smellier. Just like a good wine needs time to age, you need to let your farts ferment. They need to be cultivated … coaxed … and nurtured. Give them the time, attention, and spoiling they deserve in

this touchy feely age. Help them to develop into their full potential.

2) It will build pressure. This will allow you to do much more with the little diamonds in the roughage. It increases your versatility dramatically. For instance, you'll be able to go much longer.

3) It will allow you to be much louder, and have more control over the pitch. Best to start slow and build to adjust volume. What's the use if no one can hear you? Some comps will allow microphones, but I recommend practicing without one. If you do use one in practice, make sure you are around to watch the next person singing into your microphone for Karaoke. That's half the fun! While bubblers are great for stench and olfactory attention, they are not so good at auditory attention. The higher the pitch the better.

This travels much further, and can be heard above most noises, even in a crowded noisy environment, such as a classroom. Low pitches are good if you want to make a minor statement, but for major announcements, the higher the better. To achieve the higher pitch, you will need to practice keeping your butthole closed as tightly as you can, whilst at the same time forcing the gas through it. Done correctly, you can get them to chirp like a bird. With practice, you'll be able to play a tune. Start with something easy like *Mary Had a Little Lamb*, before progressing to challenging classics like the *1812 Overture*. It's not unusual whilst practicing the *1812 Overture*, to get successfully through till near the end, but when the cannon fire part comes in, you either a) don't have enough steam left in your pooter for proper delivery, or b) you lose control and actually fire one out the barrel.

ADVANCED TIP: Always a good idea to empty your chamber before performing in public. Never perform with a loaded barrel, and definitely never point a loaded butt canon directly at the audience.

4)   They will be much longer. Obviously the more gas you have on tap, the longer you can go for. Don't become too excited and blow your whole load too soon. Slow and steady, with enough thrust and continuous force to give a prolonged note. Advanced techniques can employ the machine gun technique...rat a tat –tat. This conserves gas, while actually amplifying the sound. Check the rules before using this in competition though, some Farting organizations don't allow this. They

say it's cheating. I beg to differ; I class it as cheeking.

If performing in the seated position, hard surfaces, such as a wooden church pew are best. This sets a hard cracking reverberating vibratory sound (vibrato) base off which to work. Soft surfaces, such as cushions, beds etc. are to be avoided. EXCEPTION: If you're naked, a leather couch or chair can really staccato out. Be sure to push down hard, so the fart bounces off the leather surface. Moisture has also to be taken into account. This can create a better seal when it's just sweat around the inner butt cheeks. However, it can be very detrimental to pitch when it's your ring that's wet. A dry butt is best for achieving the high pitches necessary to make the sound loudest. Dampness can cause a good seal of the outer cheeks though, and results in the classic "Bronx Cheer" fart. Standing posture is known as the trumpet ass position.

This really boils down to what you are trying to achieve. Do you want the distinct tone variation associated with sphincter resonation compared to cheek resonation? When doing harmony and backups, the bass baritone fart can be utilized here.

I can't over emphasize the importance of location, location, and location when it comes to sound real asstate advice…hard tiled walls and floors, such as toilets and rest rooms that provide excellent reverb, are great for extra amplification.

MORE ADVANCED TIPS

Collecting your farts for future use. Best to use a funnel and direct into a glass jar or bottle. Quickly screw the cap back on when finished, so as to not let any of the precious gas escape and be wasted.

Save jars in racks like a wine cellar. But quality criteria are the opposite of a good wine. The fart in the jar should retain its putridity, if it loses odor, and starts to go "fresh", it is "off". So don't leave them too long. Store in a cool dark place, below 25 degrees C. They do not require rotation...best left to fester undisturbed. Nothing more disappointing than selecting a 1997 bubbling Brown Shitaz or 2002 Old Fart to find it has lost its once elegant fruity stench bouquet and bite.

Made in the USA
San Bernardino, CA
15 March 2019